Living with

Beautiful

Princess

Disorder

Poems

by Camille Naomi

ISBN
Hardcover: 978-1-966565-95-6
Paperback: 978-1-966565-96-3

For myself.

"Love is a song that never ends."
-Bambi, Walt Disney - 1942

About the Author

Camille Naomi Touhet grew up in an international household; her father is French, and her mother is Singaporean. She's been writing in her journals since she first started seeing a psychiatrist in 2021, after her first panic attack. She journals her thoughts and writes poetry every day.

When she turned twenty-five, she unexpectedly found out that she was diagnosed with Borderline Personality Disorder, a fact that her psychiatrist kept secret from her and her family. All the years of questioning her emotions, sensitivity, outbursts, and suicidal thoughts finally started to make sense.

By publishing her poetry, her goal is to help others suffering and to help others know that there is beauty and hope in the world. She wishes to offer a possibility for others to relate to her words.

She also wants to help shine a light on a common mental health illness that is less spoken about, being aware that more people are being diagnosed with borderline personality disorder.

Paris

October 5th 2022

Today is my 25th birthday. It doesn't feel like it's my birthday; it just feels like an average, normal, mundane day, which is a first for me since I always cry on this 'special day.' I was diagnosed with BPD (Borderline Personality Disorder) two months ago.

These poems are not for the lighthearted…The best way to understand this is with an *open mind…an open heart.*

Contents

"BPD"

Sad girls don't eat.
We inhale pills instead; we go to sleep and
forget the world outside.
We don't want it.
Euphoric high,
Suicidal depression.
Euphoric high,
Suicidal depression.
The cycle never ends
Unless we ourselves do.

"BAMBI"

Will you hold me through the night
During my darkest times?
Ease my mind.
Tell me you love me, even if it's just for
tonight.

My wings have caught fire;
I'm falling from the sky.
Heaven has seen my sins, and I am not
forgiven.
Will you hold me when I cry?
Caress me while I stitch my back with white
ribbons.

"HER"

Delicate creature

She is.

She has a talent for turning sadness into
beauty,

Darkness into light,

Begging for forgiveness she will never receive.

There is no forgiving,

Only forgetting.

SHE IS THE WILD CARD YOU'RE
LOOKING FOR.

"MY OWN PRIVATE IDKK"

Beautiful boy,
Explorer of the world.
Look into his eyes,
Impossible not to be moved.
Fierce love, fierce passion.
He's a creature from above,
Still searching for love.
Doesn't he know?
He is the heart of all loves.
Helped save Bambi,
Helped save Me.

"TASTE LIKE HEAVEN"

From afar, it may look like I'm daydreaming.
Try to take a closer look.
My voices are spiraling in my mind,
Trying to contain whether I'm about to burst
into tears or scream.
Realizing my lungs have collapsed,
I am stuck in my loneliness.
So, I lay by the ocean, listening to the calmness
of the waves.
I take a dip in the water,
My demons are tempting me to drown myself.
Would that be so bad?
The pain my heart contains would be over.
Shh, shh, listen as the angels sing,
As I slowly swallow salt water.
My tongue can feel the tingles,
It tastes like heaven.

"ALASKA"

She doesn't look like me;
She's the complete opposite, actually:
Good Girl
Causes no problems
Good Girl.
Isn't she what you want?
Keep going; I'm about to break.
Don't get too close.
You won't see me anymore,
But please wish me upon a star.
I want to make sure you're okay.
Family and girlfriend, you're okay.
Will you come find me?
I don't belong here.

"BLUE"

In the bathroom doing coke.
I'm about to be sick
thinking about you.
Threw up all the blue,
There's a lump in my throat,
It feels kinda good.
You're not stuck on me anymore,
It's bittersweet.
"She's destroying herself," as I hear my father
whisper.

"JUST IN MY HEAD"

He says,
As I watch his wandering eyes worry,
Wishing we could skinny-dip into each other's
minds,
"Sure, let's pretend to be twin flames.
Should I call you a good friend when they ask?
Should I pretend it wasn't exciting?"
24 hours in different cities,
Nothing to lose.
Sweet boy, please don't ever be sorry with me,
Masks are off,
You know we get it.

"MARILYN"

Life imitates art.
Close up, sweetheart!
This is your big break.
Cry a little more for us darling.
She's the luckiest girl.
Beauty queen.
Smile for the cameras,
Blow a kiss for the crowd.
Her tears are real when she lies on the ground.
She went to bed and never woke up.
End scene.

"BROKEN WINGS"

Red lips, laced dress.

You like to touch my body with your dirty bare hands.

Took me to your grave; now we're descending into hell.

You looked like an angel,

Broken wings.

Did you need saving or do I continue only saving myself?

Father, please forgive my sins.

In this game of heaven or hell,

The devil will always win.

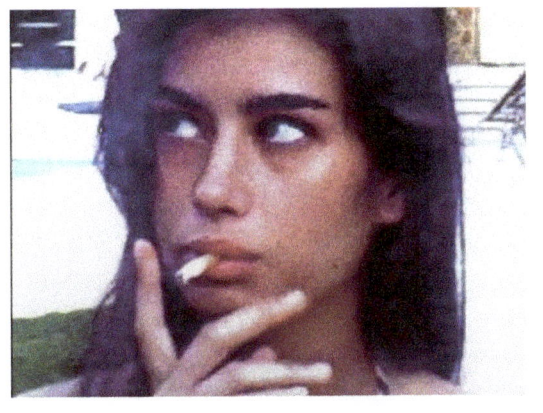

"Graveyard"

The elderly strolling through the cemetery,
Such irony.
The crows guard the caskets as the church bells
ring.
Do they know something we don't?
The autumn leaves dropping,
The wind heavily blowing,
Vines intertwined with the veins of the corpses,
Will you come visit me when my body is
decayed?
Who thought the dead could be this beautiful?
The lovers' stained glass has broken.
Running among the buried in this infinite
maze.
Will you put a rose on my tomb,
So my soul won't evaporate?

"SELF SABOTAGE"

Was it a lie when you said I was important to you?

Well, it's clear now, you want to see me go.

Why won't you say goodbye?

Don't you want to talk before I leave?

Or are you still wishing for Annie?

Why did you lie about those things?

I know that you still like her pics,

Felt like a stupid experiment.

I don't know if I'll wake up in the morning,

Mixing all these drugs till my heartbeat slows.

Don't save me; this is what I chose.

Please know it's not because of you.

My body is breaking into two,

I can't do this anymore.

Will you still think of me when I'm no longer here?

Please don't resent me for choosing this path.

I'm not here anymore,

But my heart will always be yours.

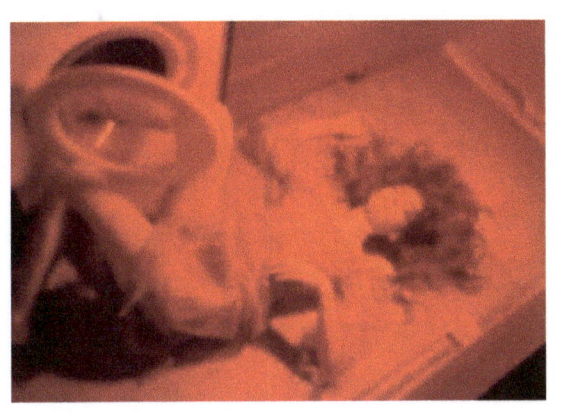

"POLISH BEAUTY"

I miss you.
You are the sunshine everyone needs,
They can't get enough of your heat.
Sweet light, I wish you could feel the effect that
people are drawn to.
You shimmer on the beach.
We are mermaids together.
It rains thunderstorms when you disappear.
Your tears pour down from the sky,
That's when we know you have left.
Come back,
We are all craving for more.

"Georgia"

Her green eyes and freckles will captivate you.
Wise beyond her years,
Trying to protect herself from this cruel world,
Her heart is pure,
Leaving a trail of flowers and peaches.
Happiness and love await her,
But I will watch after her.
I promise I will make sure.

"Oh, Deer."

My doll has been broken before,
More than once.
I would glue back the pieces together,
Except this time, I don't think I can fix her.
Oh, Deer.
It is a shame to witness her glimmer disappear,
But she was just a doll.

"Fuckboy"

He's won the game
She was unaware they were playing.
Fuckboy. Fuckboy. Fuckboy.
Said It jokingly, like the tale of Bloody Mary,
Say it three times, and she will show up,
So they say.
Fuckboy. Fuckboy. Fuckboy.
One had been in front of her this whole time.

"HOME"

I never really understood what people meant,
when they found a person they call home,
Until I met you.
You make me feel safe;
I laugh till my stomach aches.
But we're just friends.
I wish you would hold me in your arms,
I wish I could kiss your pretty mind,
I miss you all the time.
I want to go home,
Will you open your door?
Please say you will still be here.

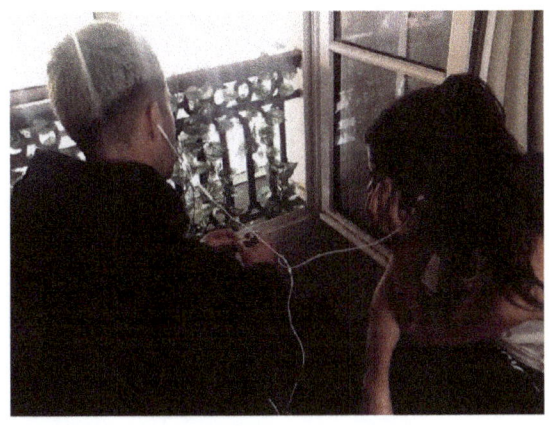

"FOREVER"

Haven't been this happy with a person.
Trying to repay you for making me smile
forever, but
I prefer sulking in my corner.
That's just what I'm used to,
I prefer being alone.
That's just what I'm used to,
To love and be loved.
Sounds like a dream I keep chasing after,
Might as well join the 27 club.
Why else would I keep it together?
I need to know you'll be good when I'm in
heaven.
Trying to repay you for making me smile
forever.

"FOR THE BLADE"

Take the razor blade and draw lines on my
thighs.
Such a high this is, you will never understand.
My body isn't a temple,
My body isn't an art,
My body is a piece from the devil himself.
Now that you know,
Welcome to my personal hell and heaven.
Knowing I'm closing my final show,
My demons are bowing into you,
They hope to see you very soon.

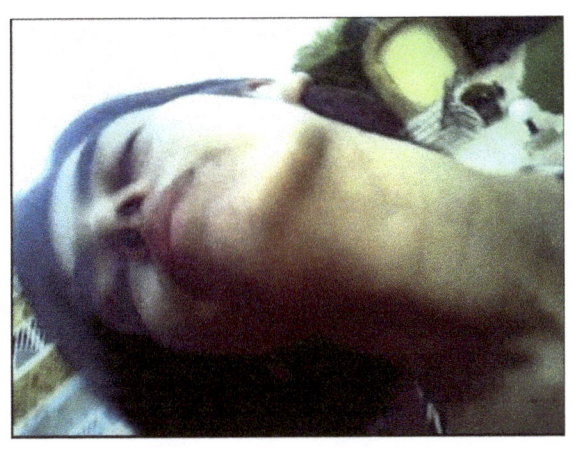

"TELL ME"

When the rain stops pouring, so will my tears.
By the looks of it, this could take years.
Maybe the sun will come out again once my
soul has burned.
I wish I could cry in his arms,
Feel his hands caress my long locks,
Telling me that everything is going to be
heavenly.
I want you so bad,
Will you see me?
Eyes deep closed in your dreams.
Will it hurt you if I leave?
I'll wait for you to bleed out so you're next to
me.

"ON OUR OWN"

I only go down on my knees for you,
Don't you see all the pretty things I do?
There's no one I'd rather obey,
You got me wrapped around your finger.
Tight.
I know I'm just seen as a mindless body,
But I don't even care,
I'd rather be taken as a fool and be close to you,
Than be violent and have you leave me on my
own.
Please don't leave me on my own.
It got violent,
We left each other on our own.

"FORMULA"

I didn't say it was anybody's fault,
It was fate that chose sadness
Over and over.
It keeps feeling like autumn,
The leaves won't stop falling,
The rain is pouring on the streets,
The white Dahlias start to look sad,
The tears keep streaming down my cheeks,
The noise of the sirens keeps going,
Until when will it all keep going?

"APART"

Do you think the universe is being fair for
keeping us
This far apart from each other?
I look at the moon, knowing you'll see it too.
Will it transfer my message to you?

"COCA COLA"

I like the taste of it,
It's as if I had swallowed a poisonous flower.
Numbing everything inside me.
Asking for more; I don't want to feel this pain.
It bears heavy on my heart.
Self-destructing in 3…2…1.

"SOUL"

*The thought of you makes my stomach turn
and twist like a contortionist.
My heart stops, and I can't breathe anymore.
The lack of attention stings.
My tears are made of diamonds.
My love has become a glass of ice.
Blew all my thirteen wishes on you,
What a waste of magic.
Can't you see that you're dating a fairy?
I'll disappear into thin air,
You'll continue to be a sad, lost boy,
Restlessly turning our wings into dust,
Your specialty.
Soon, my shimmer will fade,
You will be able to see through my skin,
Steal my bones and burn my heart,
To be kept in your trinket of past spirits and
skeletons.*

"LINES"

Did I cross the line?

When I shouted at my mama that I wanted to die?

When I asked my daddy to hide the knives?

When I dismissed my best friend's help?

Fear I might not make it to 28.

"CRETE"

Her big blue eyes reflected the same color as the ocean,
Mesmerizing every man that walks by.
Slow slips of her corona,
She awakes me from my slumber,
Says she can't handle growing older.

54

"A DAUGHTER"

I am my father's daughter.

Each time he sees me, I am a different woman.

Each time he sees me, I become a thirteen-year-old little girl again,

Raised to be his ideal idea of a lady.

Raised by my mother, she still cries herself to sleep.

Raised by my older brother, he still does good deeds.

Raised by my younger brother, he still harasses me.

Raised by myself, still protecting my heart.

"LESSON"

Is it sad that we can't have sex sober.

Has this all been a lie?

Stupid girl,

Again,

And again,

She never learns…hope haunts her.

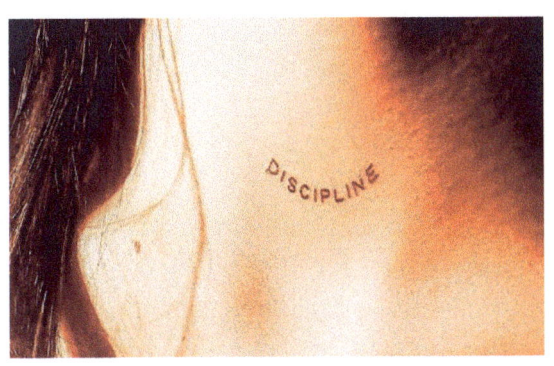

"5 AM "

It hurts my stomach swallowing it,

My nose is completely blocked.

If I kept using it that way, I would've needed a nose job.

As long as it does the same effect, that's all I want.

Numb me.

Numb my insides until I can't feel anything forever anymore.

Destroy me, I'm asking for more.

Can't you all see how well my body is handling it?

It won't let me go.

Masking the pain,

Checking my heartbeat to see if it slows,

I'm sad it doesn't.

Is that so messed up?

I ruined something so good,

It's what I'm best at.

I'm sorry if you hate me now,

You'll be more than okay.

I'll be more than okay too,

I can handle it on my own.

But how does one get off of this road?

I need angel numbers to give me hope.

"BUTTERFLY"

Finally,
She found happiness,
For herself and only herself.
She lost her way,
Started to care less,
Caterpillar turned into a butterfly.
There is hope for those who are suffering,
She is proof.
The sun rises, and she can feel the horizons
touch her face.
What a beautiful feeling that is.
Strong Stargirl.

"LOVE MYSELF"

Do you have too much pride and ego
To say that you love me too?
That's okay, that's okay,
I understand how you play.
I bet it all on you,
I lost the game, I lost the game,
And now I'm broken in two.
Tell me that it was all real and that you felt it
too.
We stopped pretending,
Slipped away,
On my own,
Now I've got nothing to lose.
I was brave,
On my own,
Now I'm pieced back into two.
I wish you were still here,
It's hard to stay sober for real.
Life is hard enough,
I just want to be loved,
Like the way I give love too.
Life is hard enough,
I had to give myself the love,
Like the way I gave to you.

"MY HEART"

In my heart, we fell in love with each other,
Didn't want to ruin what we had,
I said I love you and you ran.
Now we are both sad.
Thought we would ease each other's minds,
Beautiful chaos was created instead.
In my heart, we will get back to being friends
again,
I don't know, however, how long I can wait for
that day to come.
We wanted to be in each other's lives forever,
We were the perfect partner in crimes,
Like Bonnie and Clyde.
We would've been the best parents.
We said we were just friends,
But we fought like a couple,
Everyone else saw it.
We fucked like a couple,
Everyone else knew it.

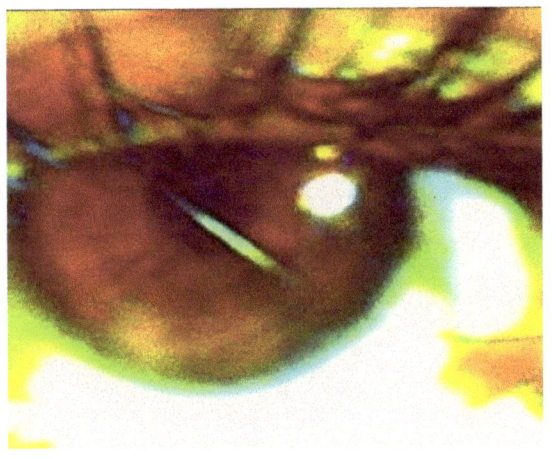

"LOVE LANGUAGE"

But that kind of intimacy should be kept in
our hearts as a secret.
I only want you for me,
I'm selfish like that.
I hate that you're not ready,
I hate that I'm not ready.
I love all your imperfections,
Special connection.
Instant.
We are lucky to have found each other,
Someone who spoke only a language we know.

"LIFE"

I'm so addicted to you,
No one has ever made me feel this high.
She gets me on another level.
If you find me looking to disappear,
You can forever seek me in wonderland.

Acknowledgments

Thank you to my parents and friends for being the best support system. I don't know where I would be without any of you here; you are always sincere and willing to help me through my darkest times. Thank you for not abandoning me and sticking through my pain with me.

Thank you to Evan Tan for taking the photos. ("Broken Wings," "Self-Sabotage," "For The Blade," "Coca-Cola," "Butterfly," "My Heart," "Life").

Hope is hard to grasp in dark times; thank you to my grandparents and my angel numbers for giving me faith.

Thank you to myself for never giving up and getting back up each time I fall, no matter how hard it stings. This book is not only for others but for me too, being a part of the industry and seeing my feelings immortalized.

"Yes, you're mad, bonkers, off the top of your head. But I'll tell you a secret, all the best people are."
-Alice to the Mad Hatter.
Alice in Wonderland, 1865, Lewis Carroll.

www.ingramcontent.com/pod-product-compliance
Lightning Source LLC
Chambersburg PA
CBHW051236120626
46547CB00013B/1665